THE MILE LONG PIANO

THE MILE LONG PIANO

First published in England, 2007 by Ragged Raven Press
I Lodge Farm, Snitterfield, Warwickshire CV37 0LR
email: raggedravenpress@aol.com

website: www.raggedraven.co.uk

© Andy Fletcher, 2007

The moral rights of the author are asserted in accordance with the Copyright, Designs and Patent Act, 1988

the mile long piano
ISBN 978 0 9552552 3 6

All rights reserved. No part of this book may be reproduced, stored in a database or other retrieval system, or transmitted in any form, by any means, including mechanical, electronic, photocopying, recording or otherwise, without the prior written permission of the publisher, except activities by the poet, or for the purpose of critical review, personal study or non-profit-making discussion.

Set in Arial.

Printed by Short Run Press Limited, Exeter, England.

Andy Fletcher

THE MILE LONG PIANO

Ragged Raven Press

for ayesha, jamil, ramiz and jessie

*and thanks to tony petch, frank newsum,
heather twidale and selma khan
for help and support*

acknowledgements:

andy fletcher's work has been published in the following magazines:

tears in the fence, bete noire, iron, resurgence, the reater, random order, different drums, proof, zenos, sepia, krax, seven days, pulse, lll, the echo room, bogg, psychopoetica, harry's hand, mutiny poems, where the barmaid pulls us milk and honey, braquemard, inkshed, iota, outlaw, illegal media, vigil

and been broadcast on ccfm radio, festival fm, bbc radio humberside

anthologised in old songs getting younger (lodge farm books), smile the weird joy, red hot fiesta and saturday night desperate (all ragged raven press)

CONTENTS

Page

9	revolution
10	small things
11	the den
12	passengers
13	meeting you
14	exhibition
16	my kooki
17	the connection
18	i shout your name
19	strong
20	the boating trip
21	tennis
22	learning
23	sorry
24	value
25	fire
26	body lotion
27	the war verandah
28	ebb tide
29	white
30	the difference
31	jellyfish
32	funeral
33	the ventilation museum
34	inflation
35	safe
36	currency
37	at the launderette
38	the white line
39	the department of birds
40	the whole valley is under water
44	pool
45	the water

46	train
47	hands
48	fifteen
49	cat sequence
50	astronomy
51	indoor fishing
52	warships
53	george w bush
54	honk
56	the u.s.a.
57	at any moment
58	sparking wine
59	man and horse
60	horse
61	football
62	long grass
63	the gap
64	jokes
65	flow
66	waiting
67	your little red shoes
68	dust trail
70	alan
72	susan
73	anne
74	writing about margaret
75	someone
76	sequence r
77	tanker
78	the bath
79	the lake
80	runners
81	the hide
82	caravan in the nettles
83	the nettles
84	on the road that goes down and up

THE MILE LONG PIANO

revolution

although
i put the chair
firmly back in its place

it keeps jiggling about

i'm worried the rest of the chairs
will get the same idea

and no sooner do i think it
than it happens

chairs tip tapping on the floor
jumping up and down

this sort of thing
has a tendency to escalate

now the curtains are at it
opening and shutting

the carpet's moving in waves

even the squat heavy sideboard
is thumping about on its stumpy feet

what a racket they're making

i should have clamped down
at the beginning

this could easily spread
from house to house
from city to city
country to country

now i know what marx and lenin
what rosa luxemburg and trotsky
were saying

as the light flashes off and on
i think
this is how it starts

small things

the real power
lies in small things.
a freckle, a ball bearing,
a dandelion seed.
a wall may stand for years
but its fall's determined
by the separation
of grains of sand in the mortar.
think of a whale relying on plankton,
a rocket beginning as a dot on a piece of paper.
a whole world's set in motion
by an eyelash, a wasp's sting,
a press-stud, a microchip.
i look at the zig-zagging reflection
of my watch on the ceiling
and at night across the darkness a shooting star.
in its path small words follow
words such as 'how' and 'why'.

the den

we didn't know
about pondichery or guadeloupe
we didn't know what 'fribbled' meant
though we fribbled about in our den
playing at buses
ding you were saying *ding ding*
we were unaware
of the north west direction of the wind
of the movement of molecules under bark
of a distant dome that was about to crack

with naked knees
we explored dark corners and moss
without understanding how bacteria
were multiplying on our sandwiches laid on a stone
without understanding the impact
of the second world war

gaps in the wall needed mud
a hole in the roof needed sticks

with no idea of my respiratory system i coughed
without being conscious of my facial muscles i laughed
we weren't concerned with eternity
the universe or god with failure or fear
only in how the sun found a way in
and made a small circle of light on the grass

passengers

at the end of the journey
the passengers refuse to get off the train

we don't want to lose our seats
they say

they sit there reading books
munching sandwiches
staying put

the police can do nothing

the carriages are shunted into a siding
and the passengers left to think
about their decision

no one leaves the train
a railway company delegation is told
we're remaining on board

days pass
weeks pass
it stops being headline news

the carriage wheels go rusty
weeds start to grow around them

a couple of passengers die
some new passengers are born

every now and then
there comes the sound of singing
from the carriages

the passengers seem immune
to the sight of trains passing
of other passengers going somewhere

meeting you

i go to the station to meet you

the train stops at the buffers
passengers with suitcases and bags get off

i look through the faces for yours

the next day
i go to the station to meet you

pigeons flap into the air as the train pulls in

people step off wave to relations
light cigarettes hug loved ones

every day
i go to the station to meet you
soon from the mass of faces
i know you'll appear and smile

years pass

the station's refurbished
old trains are replaced by new ones
timetables change

still i stand on the platform
litter blows towards me
plastic bags rise from the tracks

each day
i go to the station to meet you

exhibition

we enter the exhibition
that has no exhibits

we open the programme
to find out what's on display
but it's blank

a woman stares at a white wall
trying to see what's not there

a man's demanding his money back

it's difficult to let go of the familiar
and get involved with nothing
in the hope it'll become something

do we look higher or lower
more slowly or more quickly?

it's a question of faith
of extending beauty in all directions
beyond previous limits

a man calls to us
come over here folks
this is the moon raising its eyebrow
ah yes we say
gazing at the empty space
and beginning to see

as usual the children are quick to understand
and soon we're gathered round
'the essex dipper' which bounces about
on the floor's hard surface

next we admire 'the cerebral washing machine'
created by a woman in a black hat

we're really into the swing of it now

stretching my arms and shouting *yellow buttons*
i name my work
'dandelions growing out of an aircraft's wing'

everyone invents what they want
with no need for explanation

a latecomer arrives saying
sorry i think i've got the wrong place

no no
come on in we tell her
this is it

my kooki

everyone was at lunch
or out shopping

in between an old sadness and a future cancer
you were undressing
and i was about to become your lover

a clock struck
leaves quivered in the breeze
and as i turned away from the brightness at the window
i noticed how your ankles had been marked by your socks

you touched my cheek and called me *my kooki*
or something like that
an expression i hadn't heard before
and couldn't figure out
but kept repeating to myself

it was difficult to believe
all this had been hidden so long

everything seemed less harsh
and as you pulled up your knees
and i stroked you
i thought how inappropriate it was
that i could hear a crane banging in the distance
the dropped metal weight driving a piling home

the sound and then its echo

the connection

you lie in the bath
and i sit on a white painted chair
talking to you
running my feet over varnished cork tiles

miles across the river
under floodlights
a grab swings into the hold of a ship and lifts out coal
piles it into the shape of a cone

on this side of the estuary next to the railway
car showrooms offices and air conditioned warehouses
have neon signs saying
'mps microsoft' 'hilti' 'fast flow' 'jaguar'

near a flyover a dark and derelict 'burger king' drive-in
is now part of a travellers' site

until now
i thought us being here at this moment in this bathroom
had nothing to do with responsibility
with freedom in an unfree society
with golf and god and poverty and imagination
with the light of a star still arriving
after millions of years

you squeeze a sponge
and water sluices over your shoulders

i watch a trickle run down your arm

i shout your name

cycling alone down the track
i shout your name
at the wheat fields
at a hedge
at birds on a telephone wire
at the sky

i don't shout
for the wrong decisions we may make
for my vanity
my lack of faith
for your fear
for the hurtful things
we may say to each other
for the distance
that could grow between us

i shout
for the wind
for the sun
for your warm lips
your laughter
for a tree and its waving shadow
for the dust raised by the tyres

strong

blood rushing
to the northern part of my hand

the chair squeaking beneath us

you say *the children will hear*
a wild look that challenges monetary systems
the faces on a parade ground

your neck's salty
but we live with helplessness
with fear

in the dim light
backwards and forwards you slide
almost without moving

through nostalgia and grouted tiles
through the groans of the immersion heater
through thick dark hair

tanks cross a frontier
and a river of carnations
carries the flow of a presidency onwards

we live with belief
with choice

we gasp in spite of being afraid
to gasp

the door
on its southern eastern and western sides
is edged with light

the boating trip

i'm really enjoying the boating trip
when you point out we're not on water at all
but in the middle of a field

i look at
the grass around us
the soil stuck to the ends of the oars

i pull harder
until the rowlocks rattle and knock
until i hear the thud of waves at the bow
and spray comes over and dampens my shirt

still i row
until sweat rolls down my forehead into my eyes
until i can no longer see where we're going

tennis

i thought we'd come for a game of tennis

i serve but you hit the ball into the net

you blame the racket

i serve again but this time you just watch the ball speed by

don't you want to play? i ask

you allege i'm cheating, that i've been stepping over the base line

so you serve but when i return you call *out*

you go off after a stray ball

you don't come back

i find you behind a shed with the groundsman

i go back on court and smash ball after ball into the net, into the roller at the far end, into an adjacent court, into the conifers that surround the courts

learning

the boy kicks the ball into the bushes

the bushes from which his father has just retrieved the ball

once more his father squeezes into the bushes to retrieve the ball

he places the ball on the grass saying *this time be careful*

the boy kicks the ball into the bushes

sorry

i keep saying sorry to the carpet

the carpet doesn't say anything back

i take off my shoes
walk on tiptoe

sorry i say

the carpet just lies there with its roses
its small red squares

i try jumping across the room
but only land hard
on the carpet's edge

sorry i say again

at which point you come into the room
and ask me who i'm talking to

i look at the carpet

well? you demand

i continue looking down

you turn and say *you know*
they've got places for people like you

when you've left
i lie on the carpet
and stroke its weave

sorry i whisper *so sorry*

value

you squeeze the dye
out of a plastic bottle
massage it into your scalp
checking in the mirror
which has no memory
only the possibility of cracking
or losing its silver
you're wearing transparent gloves
and leaning over the bath
the forgetful edge where we all are
i run my fingers over the radiator
and ask if you can remember the places we've been
the times we've touched each other's faces
the occasions we've glared at one another
i say *perhaps even the moments*
we'd rather not recall have value
just like the bits we've invented
and are not able to rinse off
with a detachable shower head
obstacles that are not obstacles
a colour that'll change and change again
regardless of kisses and angry words
you comb your hair
darkness presses against the steamed up window
and neither of us knows what will remain
as water gurgles away

fire

you say you're going to leave
for someone else

in the room we painted orange
i wait for our son to fall asleep

a spider crawls across the ceiling

i hear
the other kids downstairs
playing a game

you move about in the next room

the drawer
where you keep your underclothes
squeaks as you open it

soon after we first met
we camped near a beach
made a fire of driftwood

i watched the light of the flames
on your face as we talked

here
our son stops sucking his thumb

from downstairs
the sound of the other kids
laughing

i go over to the window
to the curtains
we spent a long time choosing

i part them

in the garden
on the grass
is a circle
of charred wood and blackened bedsprings

body lotion

in the drawer
i find an unopened bottle
of body lotion

it was a present i gave you
and must have been there
for years

after a bath
or a shower
how smooth
the lotion would have made
your skin feel

i carry the bottle downstairs
unscrew the top
and pour the lotion
down the sink

the smell of it
fills the kitchen for a long time

the war verandah

on the war verandah
i'm making a speech half an inch high
into the sunset it twists
dragging an anchor across my smile
not an answer but a circle
not a pulse but a load
not a fantasy but a gaunt apology
an apple nailed to a cross
a hammer smashing the darkness
on the war verandah
the space between the rain and a telephone
finds me dodging and colluding
on a paper gallop back into history
not a pink yard but a tongue
not a dish but a forest
not a home but a blessing
stung by memory until the puzzle
becomes hard as a rail in my hand
a rail i could describe as a prayer
as a sneeze as extinction
that i could remember as a single rope
on the war verandah

ebb tide

dad plays the piano. i don't know the title of this one. the water almost disappears. not in the mud sir not in the mud. the wall light shines down on the sheet music. a jar of apple jelly awaits us. hands not weakened only weathered and a little stiff from cutting and trimming. though popular in terms of forgetfulness. his hair white. the sideburns long gone. ebb tide the title of this piece it turns out. beyond the glass dishes, cheques, bundles of illegible letters. the bass note is the mouth of a vase. the squeak of the pedal hides the softies, the ones like me. his hands sort of stroll across the keys. lunch will be ready in five minutes. cut glass. the sea reaches a point, starts to flow back again. we've come this far. i look at the wrinkles like ripples on his neck. i can't explain. an arpeggio echoes round and round a year on the way from canada to gibraltar. when his hands rise the music doesn't stop.

white

i'm painting my father white.

at the touch of my brush
his moustache twitches in surprise.

sorry dad, i murmur,
it's just something i have to do.
i don't expect you'll accept this
any more than i did when you tried
to paint me white, years ago.

i dab at him,
speckling my arms as i cover
his neck, his chest, his legs.

well that's done.
i place the lid back on the tin.
against the white woodwork
i can no longer see him.

now he won't be able to talk to me.
now he won't be able to touch me.

and yet the room still echoes
with his footsteps
as if he's walking out of the wall.

i'm just about to stamp the lid down
when i notice the brush
floating in the air.
first my feet, now my ankles
are being painted white.

the difference

by the river

i pick up a pebble
and throw it in

i hear the plop

i hear you shout

i turn round

*why did you throw that huge rock
into the water?* you ask

i start to say *it was only
a pebble*

but i notice

your hair's wet through
your clothes are dripping

jellyfish

you come in
from hanging out the washing at the back
and say
there's jellyfish in the garden

i go to the kitchen window
see them scattered across the lawn

stepping outside i take a closer look

they're in the vegetable patch too
one on top of a lettuce
another between two onions

i peer over the fence into the neighbour's garden

jellyfish there as well

back indoors
we listen to the radio news
which reports
jellyfish appearing across the whole region

an expert's saying
*no one knows where they've come from
or why*

i'm just about to start the hoovering
when our daughter runs in
through the front door
and says
there's water coming down the street

funeral

at his funeral my grandfather pushes the lid off his coffin and sits bolt upright. several mourners faint. he climbs out, steps behind the lectern and says *let's do away with time, what do you think? yeah* everyone shouts. the coffin is chopped up for firewood and soon there's a nice little blaze in the chapel. music starts and we begin to dance. grandad meanwhile is becoming younger by the minute. he's lost twenty or thirty years already and has taken up smoking again. his arthritis is steadily improving. with dancing comes trust, a coherence around chaos. grandma appears in a white dress and confetti flies through the air. suddenly the music stops. grandad's pulled out the plug. we look at him. he's only four years old. *naughty boy* someone says *you're going to get a smack*. but he jumps into the wheelchair of one of his uncles and races from the dark vestibule, out into the delirious light to the sound of bells.

the ventilation museum

the ventilation museum
has no roof

displayed in a large glass case
on the ground floor
is a hurricane

school children
prod the raging exhibit
but as our guide says
you can't poke holes in a wind

on the first floor
are gales from different eras
pre cambrian roman victorian
we feel the heat from these trapped beasts

on the top floor is the oldest wind of all
we listen to a great stillness
here all journeys come together as one

round the edges of the room are smaller cases
full of breezes and draughts

we've looked at invisibility all day
we've peered into emptiness all day
we've examined the far reaches of belief

leaving behind
our small donations to silence
we depart through doorways without doors

we step out into the noise
of the living wind in the trees

inflation

as the poet inflates himself
we hear the squeak of the foot pump

some of the air
escapes through his lips
but still he's getting larger and larger

fearing a loud bang
and being covered in dust from the ceiling
is it any wonder
we in the audience
sit with our eyes fixed on the floor

safe

what's in there behind that eighteen inch thick
solid steel door?
if i put my ear to it will i hear the barking
of a fox?
will i hear the crashing of waves driven by a force nine gale?
will i hear buds coming into leaf?
what's in there?
why such riveted strength to keep it there?
if i put my ear to it will i hear a carnival
with drums music and dancing?
will i hear two people moaning as they make love?
what's in there that it needs
a twenty five digit combination lock?
money?
bank notes?
wads of them?
am i hearing you right?
is that what you said
money?

currency

bubbles
have taken over
from money
as the unit of currency

this has the effect
of depressing the metal and paper markets
of giving a boost to soap manufacturers

tills in shops
have to be replaced
by large washing up bowls
to collect bubbles from customers
and from which to give bubbles as change

i make a hole in my credit card
so i can dip it in the mixture
and blow out however many bubbles
are required

under this new system
we realise
nothing lasts long
that even the finest rainbow coloured sphere
may burst

on tv
the director of the bank of england
is talking about huge reserves

he opens a vault door
to show us the nation's wealth
the shiny mass piled up to the ceiling

but all that's there
is empty space
and a glistening wet patch on the floor

at the launderette

i meet des at the launderette. not having seen him for thirty years. trying to match the old face to the new one. street after street covered in newspaper. his hair grey. lines around his eyes. same as me. boats embedded in mud. a spell in the army. studying sociology at the university. it's far from automatic. i don't ask if he's married in case he asks me. he tells me anyway. from a bag with a broken zip i pull sweaty shirts. how are success and failure judged? is withdrawal sought by those not in control? that ever popular drawbridge. maybe the last time i saw him we were playing football in the park. the discovery of lungs. trees blowing. before mainland solitude. he tells me he still goes to see 'city'. somehow connected by our disconnection. he says *what a place this is*. i know. trying to get things clean. trying to wash out the dirt. what time does to us. a horizon and its descendants. so many faces. *might see you here again* he says grinning as he pulls open the door to go out. sunlight on the metal top of the extractor. one by one the machines stop. the day becomes quiet.

the white line

rain starts to make longer marks on the window. the curtains have messy ends. and not only them. maggie took my hand. whip myself into shape. i was trying to. i was trying. ah yes the film. a thin white line. i was supposed to be in favour. 400 asa. half richards half jagger. or so i liked to think. but no whip and no shape. maggie smiled. the torch next to the bed is for seeing in the dark. win an award. great thing competition. no one tries to drink out of that cup. right side of the line. for every winner thousands of losers. maggie squeezed my hand hard. mould on the drain pipe. plenty of leaks. cracked paint. stay on the right side of the white line. or else. slow motion of the altamont killing. who was president then? well i suppose everyone hopes for something good. maggie was wearing her v-necked jumper. a prize nonetheless. when it's raining the birds seem to sing more. shutter speed. when the whip comes down. a different response. a different outcome. brothers and sisters why are we fighting? maggie was braver than me. kinder too. i wrote a poem called 'failure' but everyone said it failed. i was trying to. i was trying. maggie got married to an undertaker. half maggie half undertaker. sympathy for the devil. somebody must have said it. last night in the dark i couldn't find the torch. waking up with no idea of who or where or when. try 200 asa. still raining. i can see one of the birds now. a sparrow. a thin line. maggie i guess you must be out there somewhere.

the department of birds

atmospheric pollution has caused the death of all the birds in the world.

fearing the effect on the people of this country, the government sets up a department of birds whose task it is to produce and regulate replica birds. these plastic models are placed in trees and on telephone wires and are controlled from a central point. at given times during the day an operator turns a handle and the replica birds twitter and sing and flap their wings. this is so convincing people throw out crumbs for the replica birds. not wanting to rest on their laurels the development section sets to work on producing imitation nests, bird droppings and a remote controlled albatross able to follow a ship across an ocean.

of course the absence of real birds has many unforeseen consequences such as a huge increase in the rodent, grub and insect populations. the government plans to solve these problems by setting up further departments.

the whole valley is under water

the cat's caught three mice already

we have three meals a day

i don't like pears

i prefer nuts

my aunt only likes doughnuts

but then again she's bilingual

i eat apples
but i don't eat cheese

we have one tree in the garden

a bird has two wings
humans have two arms

that is some consolation

auntie has had a rest

the rest of the day goes quickly

she stays, the rest go away

she says you can keep the rest

i have made many purchases

i have bought some shoes and a mousetrap

i have bought some more nuts

there are a lot of shops in this country

the customer is always right

our cook told me her story

my love said he'd be back by wednesday

he jumped up to the ceiling

he went through the roof

i heard him swear in german

he won't be coming back

he did it for love, for me

our cook has many weaknesses
but her beauty is unusual

that is the truth

she didn't deserve what happened

she started smoking a pipe

she has a bad cold

she says she no longer supports the government
but her soufflés are still the talk of the neighbourhood

i know it's true
because i read it in the newspaper
before i go to bed
i always read the newspaper

i eat three meals a day
i do not smoke
i do not drink
so it makes no difference

the longer i stay in my job
the more stupid i get
i have to go to bed
or i'll be tired tomorrow

it can't be raining outside
the newspaper
forecast a fine night

auntie says

have you any bread?
no i haven't

have you any pears?
no i haven't

have you any flowers?
no i haven't

it can happen to anyone

i'm sitting by the fire
in the morning
in the afternoon
in the evening
i'm thinking how
the stars in the sky
have been around a long time
tears run down my cheeks
i glance in the mirror
my haircut makes me look
like pope john
i wish i was in the white lion
i nod my head
to the north
to the south

maybe life's an accident

the cook shot three birds

my auntie fired the cook

i tripped over the cat on my way to work

the apple tree has died

we're down to one meal a day

outside it's starting to rain

long live the queen

pool

in the pool
she creates the only human sound

her feet and ankles shine

she knows he's watching from the balcony
that he sees things differently
as men do

can he hear
the whispers of moving water?
does he understand what they mean to her?

she's gone past drowning
past remembering

his way is tried
and diminished by trying

hers is an underworld
of blurred edges and heavy echoes
marked not by moments or years

but by waving blue tiles

in the past it's always the same
in the future it could be different

as she surfaces
through bursting colonies of lost kisses
the sun flashes on a stainless steel rail

unlike him
she has no desire to control

she hasn't looked up to the balcony
to see if he's still there

lying on her back
she floats
she listens

the water

you take off your clothes
put on your costume
dive into the water
into that country of bubbles
where voices are hard to decipher
you breathe in
left arm right arm
married or single winning or losing
away from a violent memory
not connected to the paleness of the day
away from what he doesn't or didn't or will not do
a house seems certain by comparison
but a comparison with what?
not the light catching on the wavering surface
or that grotesque face coming towards you
the water in the gutters at the edge
finds its way back into the pool
so you can dive again
beyond the traffic
to something that's closer and more real
to a part of you that's unhurt
and within reach
a sharp or flat altering the scale
the minor chord becoming a major one
and wherever he is you let him continue talking
to the woman whose wardrobe is jammed
who's lost the key
you pull yourself out of the pool
and return to the cubicle
breathing out
breathing in
knowing these walls can't contain you
that you'll step out into a street
that leads to other streets
out into the cold wide sunlight

train

from his room
he watches
a train on the embankment

flat trucks loaded with steel

he's a long way from home
from the station where he said goodbye
to his mother and his sisters

the flat trucks roll by

he remembers the hugging
the shouts
the waving

that was when the trees
had lost their leaves
and the tracks
were two dark lines in the snow

the steel trucks pass and are gone
the leaves of the trees on the embankment
stop fluttering

here
there are other families
people coming home from work
school

in this strange country
he lets the net curtain fall

in the distance
he hears the throbbing of the locomotive

hands

your hands shake as you lift the dish out of the oven. a fork leaves holes in the potatoes. why here of all places? the refrigerator hums. mist on the coast. who's that climbing the fence? retaliation. bombs. whispering in the bedroom. the peas are not quite done. stop at the police station on the way and see if there's any news. don't you dare do that. bikini. atoll. what? man's work. woman's work. i start to think i know nothing about what's happening. my hands departed long ago. a 1960s dormer bungalow. the care taken. the love given. the carrots ready. spots in the eyes when it comes to the royal family. the shades of gravy. phew it's hot in here. we all look so much younger for a moment. better without the burden of expectation. it felt as if the sea embraced me. cold. your hug warm in the dunes. lift off the pan lid. the hedge gets thicker the trees taller. open the door and let some air in. a way of coming to terms with hands. at the open kitchen door coloured streamers ripple in the wind.

fifteen

in the cloakroom at school
i kissed a boy full on the lips

i was fifteen
and we'd have done it again
if we hadn't been caught

i used to imagine him
swollen with boredom
his nakedness a parachute on which
he descended from a deep blue sky

afterwards
i had to wear a jacket of shame
listen to calls of 'homo' and 'queer'

i couldn't separate truth from truth

i crept away into an innocent forest
where coats hung
from the branches

the big muscled boy
with soft skin
would appear round a tree trunk

and we'd reach for each other
and kiss and kiss and kiss

cat sequence

the cat and i are watching football on television. between the gasps of the crowd she purrs and stretches her claws. just after half-time i realise i don't care about the match, who's playing or what the result is. the real game finished hours ago, the floodlights are cold and litter swirls around the terraces. i open the door. there are an estimated four million cats in britain. some have an ear or leg missing but few relish being put out at night, and this cat is no exception. with a warm corner in mind she scrambles upstairs. no amount of sucking noises or high-pitched pleas can entice her from the silence under the bath, a cast iron victorian model with an overflow that hasn't been connected. i lift off the hardboard side-panel - dust, a shampoo bottle, mouse-droppings, a heap of silver solder and some pebbles the kids brought home from the sea. the scene evokes the inside of my head - the stuff that's hidden for years and is found only by chance. no cat, but i hear my grandmother telling me that during the war when searchlights scissored the sky, she believed a torch could reveal the location of manchester to enemy planes a thousand feet above. she never had a cat. neither did my father though his mother wore a ukrainian fur hat. but he still knew that it was a man walking in a november fog who'd observed and then 'invented' 'cat's eyes', but it puzzles this estimate of the number of cats in britain. who does the counting and how? it can't be done by heads, or tails. perhaps it's based on the number of tins of cat food sold divided by the amount the average cat consumes. the average cat? well sleep becomes necessary sooner or later - floodlights and air-raid sirens get swallowed by yawns and the alarm clock's ominous tick. i abandon my search in the way that searches are often abandoned - without finding what i was looking for, or thought i was looking for. falling asleep, my consciousness begins to crackle, loses its vertical hold, crosses the decades, while footballers with green eyes and slinky limbs still aim for that elusive goal.

astronomy

a galaxy, clean, healthy and free from blemishes
is not one perpetuated by schedules
nor by sanitary appliances and cisterns made of
wood nineteen millimetres thick.
the bower barff process takes us a long way
from dense dust clouds, the vortex
in which bits of food, soap scum, mothers,
hedges, clouds and fire engines disappear.
we represent this as

$$d + 4.7 = m - w \times 349.9$$

the surface of each star has a rich texture,
a bloom from which the oldest florets
have been removed. the heat loss which makes
an irritating noise in the back boiler
isn't helped by judgment, for then, dog collars,
railway sleepers, toe nails, grand pianos,
doves of peace and wallets have to be
considered.
we represent this as

$$r = 8.3 \times 10k \, (b + f)$$

analysis of density and mass leads to
estimates of size, but for maximum beauty
horrid stains should be removed with the finger-
tips. from this activity a tough, horny, flexible
surface emerges which can be seen
in relation to motorways, plate glass windows,
catfood, ear-rings, no smoking signs and owls.
we represent this as

$$\frac{6m}{l} = t \times 445.66$$

it has to be admitted that our knowledge of
astronomy is far from complete.

indoor fishing

fishermen
crouch over a bath
in the middle of a room

indoor fishing
means they don't get wet when it rains
don't have to put on layers and layers of jumpers
when it's freezing cold

in typical fashion
one of them lands an old boot
one of them reels in a length of weed

everything's going fine
until someone hooks the bathplug

now they know
there'll be no fish today

that it's time to go home

warships

the rubber warship heads out of port

the sailors on board
are happy
because they know their ship can't sink

an enemy warship
also made of rubber
sails from an enemy port

its sailors too
are happy
because they know their ship can't sink

both crews are fully aware
that rubber warships only fire rubber bullets

the politicians however
are making threatening noises
about what they're going to do to the other side

it's in every paper
on each tv channel and radio station

everyone's talking about the mighty impending battle

out in the atlantic
the warships ram each other
bounce off
ram each other again

the captains and crews
are having the time of their lives

george w bush

george w bush
has been wrapped in clingfilm

and put on display
in the exhibition

several people have got angry
and tried to knock him off his pedestal

somebody's tried to peel off the film

now a uniformed guard's
been placed beside him

it's not easy to tell it's george
though the greying hair
and pink skin
certainly look like him

his shape is so much softer
it's hard to imagine him
invading iraq
or refusing to sign the kyoto treaty

did those squeezed lips
really say *terrorist*
and *weapons of mass destruction*?

the clingfilm has made his suit shiny
made him look like a crooner
from las vegas

or a pale resident
from a nursing home

in fact he could be anyone

honk

honk
manchester birdie ho ho
manchester drizzle ping
an argument ringing in wires
no smiles across a thousand miles
shoot out at supper
smooth fears skol cheers
rostbiff good biff
jaw jaw the nervous system
jelly legs
honk
new york birdie ho ho
new york airport ping
you socked me with a right good left donna
the merry go round's too fast
it can't last
my stomach's a stunning ragu
made from a sardine
found inside a condom
honk
turin birdie ho ho
turin acapella ping
take a lot off
not too short
introducing medicine that will
release the bitter self tightening waistcoat
an offer not to be missed
here come the buttons
honk
tokyo birdie ho ho
tokyo restaurant ping
you're using an inhaler to inhale yourself
your beautiful self
ah salve for saliva
a plaster over your gob bob
a flask full of flowers
as a joke
from the bloke in 3b

honk
moscow birdie ho ho
moscow hot borsch ping
the classes are small
the children smaller
but if you don't listen to what's said
of course you'll end up in morse
as the cable tightens
feeling frightened
of the man with the machine gun laugh
honk
rotterdam birdie ho ho
rotterdam refinery ping

the u.s.a.

the united states
has been relocated
to the isle of wight

most of the island
is taken up with new york
and its skyscrapers

the rest of the country
has had to be sawn off
and left to sink into the sea

where
are the deer and the antelope
to roam?
where
can the six lane super highways go?

the traffic
drives round in circles
the farmers have nowhere to farm
and the president
finds himself sharing a room
in a guest house in sandown

on the payphone
he manages to get through
to one of his government officials
who tells him that just one direct missile hit
and the u.s. could be gone

will the americans
change their ways?
start to walk instead of driving?
conserve instead of consuming?
give up
threatening
invading
waging war?

the world looks on

at any moment

at any moment
the universe may turn itself inside out

and then where would we be
with our carrier bags full of bargains?

sparking wine

a mal lact fermen wi gi yo a spar win acci a wer bu i i eve mor fu to mak on deli. al you nee, a suit mus – app, pea, goo, rhu arr a id ingre. a champag, yea, an no to muc sug thi t dryn, rac twic, matu fo abu, six mots, an en ottle i champag botts, add t eac leve oon o sug an a lit menti champag, yea. cor wel wit a tru linder cor win an wir i cure. ture fo a east tree onth. do no mak i win in nary ottles – hey, eve, crew topper an yo ends an lati wil i i oo ecla abs terrif.

man and horse

a man is leading a horse across the sea. he walks on the waves, stepping from the top of one to the bottom of the next. the horse leaves hoof-prints which swirl and quickly disappear. the wind ruffles the horse's mane, blows the man's hair across his face. i could be the man or the horse, the man in a grey jacket and worn boots, the horse with a bare patch on one of its flanks. i could even be the rope connecting them, a wet rope with a few frayed strands. spray whips off the crest of a wave and dampens my face, leaving a salty taste. i don't know how far the man and the horse have come or how far they've left to go but at this point there's no land in sight. they plod on, stumbling occasionally but continuing nonetheless.

horse

it starts with 'horse'
which becomes 'big horse' or 'little horse'
'big black horse' or 'little brown horse'

at some point
a fence is put round the horse
'strong' or 'plodding' are allowed
'whistling' or 'polite' are not

but on the other side of reason
a horse uses cutlery
jumps out of a cloud
gallops across the head of a dandelion

if fields dance
fences collapse

ride the brain bareback

you can travel miles

there's no horizon
no end

football

football's more popular than religion. the willow tree's pony tails swish in the wind. why are spaces where they are? the light cuts across the framed photograph of our daughter. the rough guide to italy. the smooth guide. a guided missile. only her face can be seen. the sound of the television from the front room. argentina versus the ivory coast. the slightest movement of air sets off the windchimes. the things we buy. the people we love. a picture behind a picture. we can follow the guide but it may not take us where we want to go. a good thing there aren't wars fought in the name of football. the light fades. a gap in the picture rail. a gap in time. our daughter comes downstairs singing to herself. the crowd howls for a penalty. to know a room by its shadows. to have nowhere to go nothing to do no one to be. a missile explodes. the sound of sobbing. no need to draw the curtains. the referee's whistle heard through the cheering. what if there is no guide? our daughter runs upstairs again. how many pictures? the tinkling of the windchimes.

long grass

in the long grass
a lorry
with no windscreen
no seats
no steering wheel
no tyres

i wondered with had happened to the lorry

in the chair
my grandmother
with her skin wrinkled
her hands folded
her mouth open

i wondered why my grandmother didn't speak to me

my father took me by the hand
led me out of the room

led me
past the long grass
to a ridge overlooking a motorway
where the traffic roared
to the north
to the south
on and on

the gap

you jump across the wooden boards of the pier

the shadow of your blowing hair jumps with you

through a gap in the planks
we look at the swirling water

three years old
you ask *what's down there?*

i think
fish
a buckled pram
keith richards cranking out the opening chords of 'jumpin jack
                                                                        flash'
an explosion way back in time
a teenager afraid of everything afraid of nothing
a hole where mice dart in and out
a scene from a tarkovsky film in which barn doors blow open
                                  to reveal a bricked up entrance
my mother whispering words i can't decipher
the sun glinting on points at a railway junction
thousands of wind turbine blades rotating
an old man who's chained himself to the railings

instead of answering
i squeeze your hand
knowing whatever you see will be different to what i see

look i say as we continue to gaze down between the planks
at the surface of the swaying water
at the bubbles
the sparkling light
look

jokes

why is a car like a chicken?
because it's a biscuit

why is a tree tall?
because it's not a tree

you didn't even come up
to our waists
when you told your jokes
that no one understood

but you laughed
with your mouth
your eyes
your hair

and we chuckled too

now you're 13 stones
and 6' 4"
and when i remind you of those jokes
you don't get them either

why does the cat say miaow?
because it's a frying pan

we sit
and look out at the rain
as it slides down slates
makes a detour round a piece of moss
before dripping into the gutter

we both burst out laughing

flow

your hand on the railing
of the footbridge
you used to jump from

jump
it's astonishing
how far back we can go

to your baby eyesight
my green shirt
as breathless on a battered sofa
i held you

morning
eighteen years later
the sky a masterpiece of blue
we walk down a hill
to reach the water
to stand above it

our reflected faces wobble
your hair waves in the current
your presence spreads wide

we laugh
as we throw sticks
that bob and spin
until they're caught or slip out of sight

you cross the footbridge ahead of me
and it's hard not to think in clichés
but who you'll be
is who you believe
who you imagine
who you create

on the other bank
with your foot
you release water
blocked by mud and dead leaves
silver and rushing
to join the flow

waiting

evening. i wait for you to come out of your class. the sound of singing. a piano. waiting allows me to pass from one year to another. a security camera mounted on the wall. grass growing out of a gutter. no such thing as the clear flow of the past. no sign of you yet. a new song begins. it's said practice makes perfect. yet i often give up almost as soon as i've started. i can make of this whatever i want. maybe it's true there's nothing more frightening than freedom. i recognise this song. it ends with cheering and stamping. you have the beauty of being young. of believing everything's possible. i shift from one foot to the other. as time goes by my actions seem to get smaller. another parent clicks her tongue. *how much longer?* she says. there's a certain power in what's lost. some parents have gone inside. why am i standing outside? a siren in the distance. you know i would wait and wait and wait for you. until you appear scowling or smiling with a bag over your shoulder. compartments of thought even in the open air. eventually there's no such thing as keeping. one of the parents comes out and says *they're on the last song now*. i look up past the security camera. past the gutter. the voices rise. two birds fly off together. the sky's a deep blue.

your little red shoes

i see you

in the field where the blade of a plough has left the earth
cut and shining

in the enclosure where two horses nuzzle and flick their tails

in the playground where an empty swing sways in the wind

dust trail

a dust trail up a track between fields

harvest time
no rain for a week
a farm labourer driving fast

he's thinking about his girlfriend
with no clothes on
the things she does to him

he presses the accelerator to the floor

the wheat's thick
on either side
he can still hear
his father's shouted obscenities

later there'll be rabbits to shoot
as a square in the middle of a field
gets smaller and smaller

there'll be a weasel to pick up
by its tail and nail to a barn door

there'll be beer to be drunk

i see his face as his van
shoots under the bridge
over which the train i'm on is passing
the 17.25 intercity diesel
from london kings cross to hull

i've been making notes
trying to pick out a few phrases
from a storm of words on a page

we both think we know where we're going
he has a meeting with his boss
i have a printed destination on my ticket

we're far away
from where decisions are made
where a map's divided into economic zones
where a cathedral and tower blocks rise

forces that seem beyond our control
are moving us
though we try to reclaim what we can
on our own terms

i think about it again
i could be behind his steering wheel
he could be in my seat

fumes from the van and the train
mingle for a moment
before dispersing

he stops and climbs out of the driving seat
grins at the farmer

i hold out my ticket to be inspected

we move further and further apart
the dust settles on the verges
on the tall swaying grasses

but words and thoughts
hang in the air
and won't be still

alan

we stand
at the traffic lights
waiting to cross
even through my coat
i can feel
the grip of your fingers
you say
you're not twenty one
any more
these days
your clothes can walk
and there's holes in you
through which
anyone can step
you put your hands
across the clock
to stop it shrinking
across the eyebrows
of accountants
solicitors
this land is their land
you and an old baseball cap
a stick
an unshaven face
shaped from
years of trying
your body in a blaze
of alcohol
the scarlet of belief
breakfast would be
a big success
the ringing
from a public call box
could be your ex-wife
disgusted at mouse droppings
crusted pans
you remember her laughing
a tennis ball

bounced and bounced
on your racket
before the laces
wriggled free of your shoes
we stand
at the traffic lights
in the rain
the wind
even through my coat
i can feel your fingers
holding on

susan

in your room
you slump in your wheelchair

you don't speak
you can scarcely turn your head

it's hot

a drop of sweat
runs down inside my shirt

at the end of the visit
i go out into the cold

i cycle to the edge of the city

along the track
hawthorn leaves and berries
have fallen

across the blue sky
a plane leaves a vapour trail

i stop at a bridge over a river
and think of you again

i want to shout out loud
but the quietness of the bare fields
overwhelms me

i look down at the murky water

anne

in the front room sunlight sparkles on the windowledge. being home is one thing. i'm thinking about anne from the office who said she'd be back at work in a day or two. whatever it is that takes us closer. dust particles rising when i sit down in the chair. being in a strange place is another. an amusement arcade. i pull the arm on a one armed bandit. one plum one lemon one orange. far from our desks and gill saying *it's going to take longer than anne thinks*. the air made visible. whatever it is that takes us further away. bandit. rogue. gill telling us how anne's hair is coming out in handfuls. no one speaking. gill leaves the meeting in tears. the door squeaks on its hinges. rouge is no use. one apple one orange one lemon. a one in how many chance? coins tinkling in the metal tray. smoke coming out of the chimney shows the direction of the wind. three children. eight grandchildren. being nowhere is hard to imagine. a cloud changing shape before breaking up. only in strong light do i see the scratches on the glass. anne smiling. whatever it is that takes us beyond.

writing about margaret

margaret was born in hull in 1917 and has lived there all her life. for several years she worked in a chemicals factory – a small, bright-eyed woman who's always tried to make the best of things. her only regret is that she never managed to have any children. after her husband died, she went to live with her brother, then her niece, now she lives in a residential home on the edge of the city.

this was how i began. then i stopped and asked –

>who is margaret?
>what do i know about her?
>what does she mean to me?
>would she approve of my writing about her?

even if i could have answered these questions, i would still have had to decide whether to write in poetry or prose, in the first or third person, in an imagist or realist idiom. (writing about people is like putting a frame around them and i still don't know how to resolve it).

in the end, i decided that the whole thing would be better in the form of a sociological/biographical essay. but this was not a task i wanted to undertake.

i was left with the scattered bricks of a poem, a list of words i'd planned to use

>urine
>armchair
>hyacinth
>bread
>terrace
>bunting
>acid
>smile
>hopscotch
>curtain
>cry.

someone

he moves
coins tobacco a lighter
from one pocket to another

he moves
a newspaper a margarine tub
a packet of biscuits
from one carrier bag to another

and this goes on for hours

no-one sits on the bench near him
people walk past
and find somewhere else
to talk about the sunset
the light on the waves
the boats coming and going

from a safe distance
they watch him remove a pair of trousers
to reveal another pair underneath

something like skin
something like pain
something like birth

as if he could become someone else
he carries the trousers
down to the water
and throws them in

there's something of how
the people feel about him
in the way the trousers don't drift off
but float back to the shore

sequence r

rain
drips
from
the
tall
metal
railings

i
didn't
know
i'd
never
see
you
again

rain
drips
from
the
tall
metal
railings
darkening
the
concrete
below

tanker

i pull back the curtains to find an ocean-going tanker down the length of the street. i get dressed and go outside to have a look. several of the neighbours have gathered to stare at the mighty vessel. no one knows where it's come from. no one knows how it got here. its sides have flattened the garden walls. we can see the rivets and barnacles on the hull. one woman says *we don't want it blocking our street*. a young man disagrees *hey think of the free oil - and the money we'll get from the tourists*. i put up my hand and gaze at the bridge. no sign of any crew though smoke's curling from the funnel. we walk round to the stern. the ship has no name, no port of registration. there's a breeze strong enough to blow my hair coming from the spinning propellers. old tom from no 52 nods his head. *i used to be a sailor so i quite like having a tanker here*. a little girl says *maybe it's always been here but we've never seen it before*.

the bath

grass grows
up through the plughole
of a bath at the end of the lane

there are no taps
no pipes connecting it
to the mains supply

there are no floorboards underneath
only a pile of soil and rubble
on which the bath tilts
so rainwater full of tiny wriggling creatures
collects at one end

if only i could disconnect myself
in the same way

if only light from many angles
through the overhanging branches
could fall on me

the lake

if the lake were a mirror
the oars would scratch
if the lake were a dictionary
the oars would drip with words
if the lake were a forest
the oars would get tangled

it's easy you say *easy like this*
in out
in out

or look at it
from the lake's point of view
the underside of a boat
sliding across its skin

that overhanging branch
watch out

stay on the water
the air the rhythm the music
faith will repay our staying on board

it's easy you say *easy*

if the lake were sky
we would drift and drift

runners

the runner dies while running. we receive an invitation to her funeral. the instructions she's left are that people should attend in shorts and singlets and have to get to the church by running. the relatives from out of town arrive exhausted but there's no let up. during the service we have to run on the spot which creates a terrific racket and makes us breathless when we try to say a prayer or sing a hymn. instead of the usual sniffing and sobbing there's the sound of panting the smell of hot bodies the dripping of sweat on to the pews. but we've learned something from our dead friend. with the pounding of feet still in our ears we run out of the church into wind and driving rain and don't stop.

the hide

a pile of dogshit at the top of the wooden steps. one
step is covered in melting tar – more alert than i am –
little bubbled eyes taking it all in. a track leads to
a hide at the side of a lake. i open a flap, let in
light. ducks swim across dazzling water. each time i
blink another year passes. graffiti reads *haven
gang rule* and *i have big breasts*. who's written it? i
close the flap, the graffiti retreats into the grain.
the girl with big breasts unfastens her bra while her
boyfriend can hardly breathe, shut inside the darkness,
sweaty, sticky, forgotten ecstasy for me, for them,
climbing back up the steps where dog has not yet
defecated. ducks swim across the lake at night, a
century of ducks becoming smaller, returning to their
shells, the eggs sealing, the eggs still inside the
mother duck. the boy tries to control his spurt, the
night's sprayed with stars. in the still soft tar, the
girl leaves a footprint. why is so much beyond the
reach of steps, beyond understanding? a dinosaur egg.
an egg out of which a planet hatches in the reeds, a
nest which the boy picks up and hurls as far as he can
shouting *fuck you*. the sound travels along a railway
line, telephone lines, a line of latitude. *you're a
silly bastard* says the girl, laughing at the top of
the steps which haven't yet been built. she turns her
head, her hair into the wind.

caravan in the nettles

the door off its hinges

dead leaves on what's left of a cushion

your folded sunglasses still there

nobody's ever asked me and i've never told them

the nettles

we're on the move
using moonlight as memory
across an orchard a railway yard
a car park

we're hated by you
we're kicked we're hacked
we're set on fire by you

yet still we inhabit your dreams
pushing out of
a pillow out of a mattress
our dark green heads thrust
through a carpet through floorboards
through solid concrete

you're too closed to be free
you're even scared of your own protection
property and wealth are your units of measurement
your luxury is faithless
and full of nothing

but we have roots
we're packed with gentleness and pain
our death feeds our children
in the exact moment of their beauty
the loneliness of each stem
is overcome by our community our sameness
the tossing of seeds
each season has its own dignity
and passes to the next

we climb mountains
we wave from the tops of the highest buildings
we sting the sky
and bring out a rash of stars

on the road that goes down and up

this is the sort of car i've always wanted.
one with no engine.
where are we heading? you ask
as i twiddle with the rusted gearstick.
if i knew the answer i'd tell you.
i stare at grass growing out of the dashboard.
now's the time
to follow feelings of love and desire
to maintain an open mind and forget about results.
on the road to the ideal
some adjustments may have to be made
and the responsibility's with us.
slow down a bit you tell me
we're going far too fast.
i press gently on the dock leaf
that serves as a brake pedal.
it's marvellous to have no wheels
and be travelling so smoothly
but i've no idea how long we can keep extending time.
soon the motorways may be covered
in weeds and bushes
and we'll have to fit our entire belongings
into the glove compartment.
you climb into the back
and poke your head
out of the window with no glass.
through a crack in the plastic seat
you can see all the way to wales,
waves flashing along its coastline.
as we ride we realise the journey's
as important as the destination,
that endings are often not perfect
and may judder on a bit.
i reach for the ignition key
but it's been replaced by a snail.
how different things are from when we started.
light flickers over our skin.
above us, the wind ripples in leaves.

Ragged Raven's recent poetry publications:

The Invention of Butterfly by Christopher James
£7   ISBN 978 0 9542397 9 4
...a wonderful eye for an image and a wonderful sense of humour. **Orbis**

Kung Fu Lullabies by Chris Kinsey   £7   ISBN 978 0 9542397 7 0
An array of miscellaneous, very enticing poems exuding originality. A most rewarding exprience to read. **New Hope International**

Seven League Stilettos by Jane Kinninmont
£7 ISBN 978 0 9542397 6 3
The whole feel of the book had a spark of something that was special ...pictures that could not be caught with a camera. **Reach**

Vanishing Point by Tony Petch   £6.50   ISBN 978 0 9542397 3 2
...throughout the book there are flashes of genius as insight combines with surprising expression. www.suite101.com, **Cold Mountain Review**

People from bones by Bron Bateman and Kelly Pilgrim
£6.50   ISBN 978 0 9542397 0 1
Two poets who tackle life with wit and sympathy ...Together they have created an excellent collection. **New Hope International**

the cook's wedding by John Robinson   £6.99 ISBN 978 0 9520807 8 7
A poet with immense talent, a poet at war with himself. **Voice & Verse**
Accessible, visual and rich. **The New Writer**

When pigs chew stones (anthology 2007)   £5   ISBN 978 0 9552552 2 9

The White Car (anthology 2006)   £5   ISBN 978 0 9552552 0 5
Some subtle and lovely work...another great collection. **Poetry Monthly**

Writing on Water (anthology 2005) £5 ISBN 978 0 9542397 8 7
The hallmarks of the entire collection are strength, versatility, integrity and a bold fusion of highly complex emotions and rigorous intellectual questioning. **Cold Mountain Review**

Saturday Night Desperate (anthology 2003) £5 ISBN 978 0 9542397 2 5
A whole host of good things...emphasising the excellence of contemporary poetry today...You'll read it again and again. **bluechrome**

The promise of rest (anthology 2002)   £5   ISBN 978 0 9520807 9 4
This is one of those anthologies where you don't look for what's good, but what is exceptional ... an excellent collection. **Purple Patch**